AF580349

Appreciate the Fingerskate

Appreciate the Fingerskate

by

Ashley Davis

Printed in the United States of America

First Printing, 2022

ISBN: 9798368071510

This book is dedicated to all the readers of Flippin' Out. I really enjoyed getting to write about something I love. Thank you for your support. It means the world.

Introduction

Fingerboarding started in the 1960s, and it's been around ever since. Since its invention, fingerboarding has become more than just a fun pastime or something for kids to do. It has made its mark worldwide with competitions across the country and internationally and has been deemed a sport.

Still, there are varying views on fingerboarding both positive and negative. Regardless of other people's views, anyone interested in fingerboarding can decide for him or herself whether it is worthwhile.

There are all kinds of fingerboards that can be found at several stores and online. Decks can be customized just like skateboards. Sometimes you can find a fingerboard deck that matches your skateboard deck.

There are standard fingerboards, low-end fingerboards, and high-end fingerboards. The prices vary, the sizes vary, and the materials vary. Fingerboards can be extremely thin, wide, long, short, or a combination. Some are built to be more durable than others. The larger boards are sometimes easier for people with larger hands to use. However, you won't know what fingerboard feels comfortable until you test it.

Fingerboarding is basically what you make of it. It can be fun and relaxing, or it can be stressful and frustrating. Landing everything and learning every trick are not easy things to do. The board will shoot out from underneath your fingers. You will over or under flick the board which could end up launching it somewhere you did not want it to go. You could finally land a trick clean for the first time, and your board might break. A lot of things can happen, but the feeling of successfully landing makes all of those things worth it for a lot of people. Landing tricks by mistake is pretty common when trying to get the feel for fingerboarding, but there are some tricks that are easy to learn when using a fingerboard for the first time.

For example, rolling down stairs is an easy way to work on Firecrackers.

Other easy tricks are Manuals, Nose Manuals, Hippie Jumps, and Body Varials. Learning some baseline tricks is a great way to get the process started before working on harder tricks. To avoid getting bored with those tricks, putting them together to create combos can be effective.

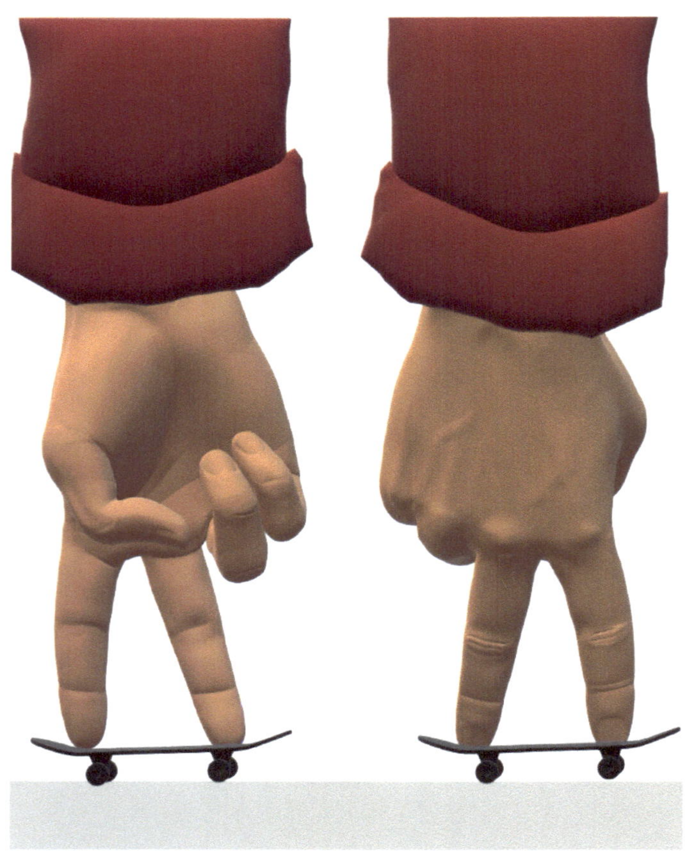

Shuvs are a great way to get used to the board rotating and to learn how much pressure to put on the board with your finger to avoid under and over rotating. They are also a trick that can be done without learning how to Ollie.

One of the most important tricks to learn is the Ollie. Having a solid Ollie helps to avoid random tricks. It also makes learning a lot of tricks easier. The higher the Ollie, the more time you have to allow the board to rotate and/or spin in different directions.

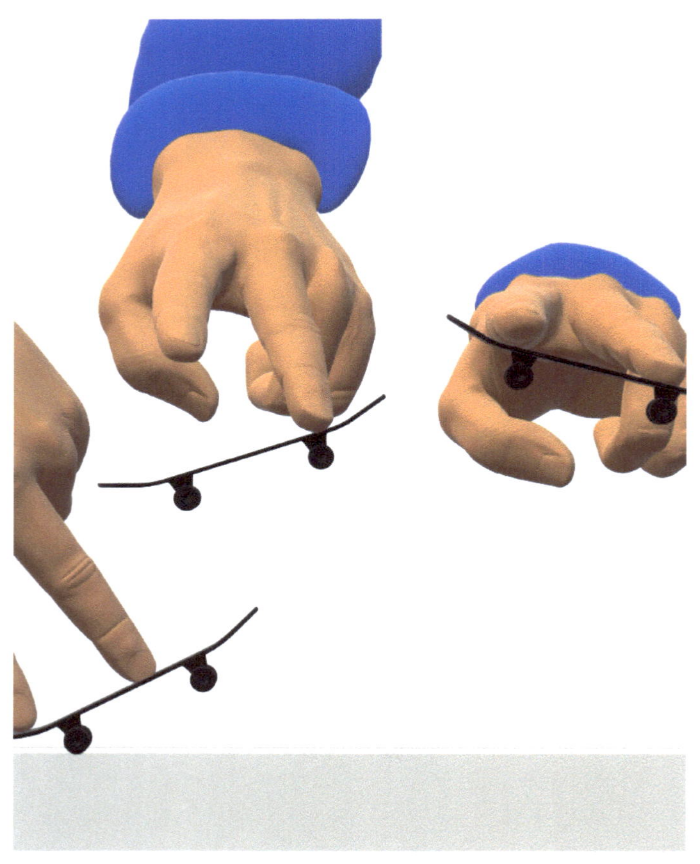

Many fingerboarders have different ways of doing Ollies. Some roll forward, bring the board backward, and pop the tail to achieve an Ollie. Others pop the tail, rotate their wrists so the board is laying upside down on their fingers, and rotate their hands forward to Ollie. Different ways work for different people, but once you master your technique, the results are often the same.

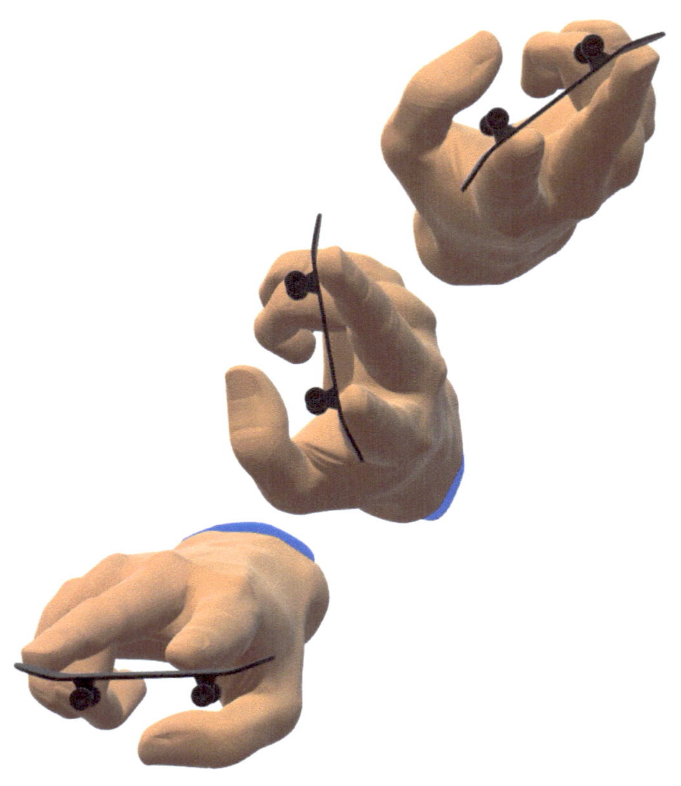

After learning how to Ollie, tricks like Kickflips and Heelflips will become far easier. The slightest shift of your front finger will affect which way your board rotates. The higher the Ollie, the longer you will have to make your board rotate, so practicing good, consistent Ollies is key.

The process of learning new tricks can be time-consuming and at times frustrating. If you are struggling and becoming annoyed, go back to what you know and add the new things you have learned. Eventually, you will land new tricks if you do not give up. In the process, you might even land something unexpected.

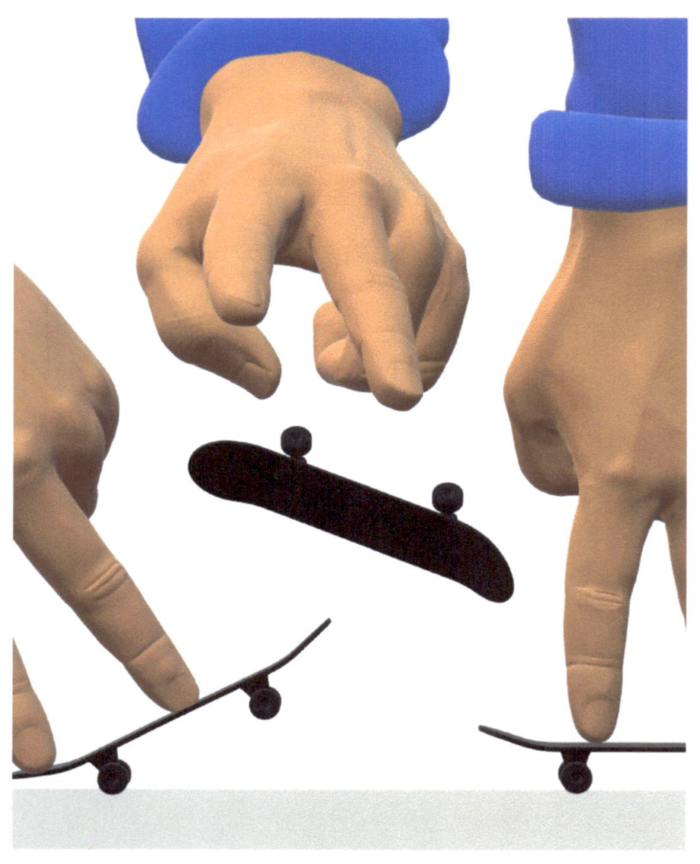

As your Ollies get smoother and higher, using different obstacles whether handmade, storebought, or non-fingerboard related will help you to get accustomed to holding your Ollies for extended periods of time.

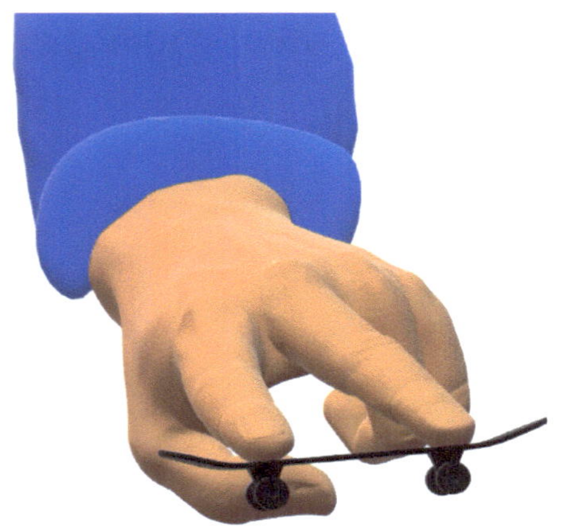

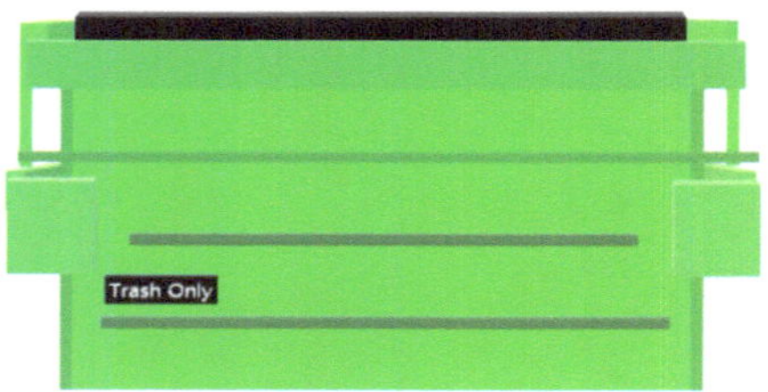
Trash Only

Another fun but sometimes challenging thing to do is learning Nollies or Nose Ollies. It can feel very awkward and unnatural because your wrist, hands, and fingers are not accustomed to the movement. Learning Nollies can require a substantial amount of patience because it can take longer than learning an Ollie. An easier way to begin learning Nollies is practicing Nollie Shuvs.

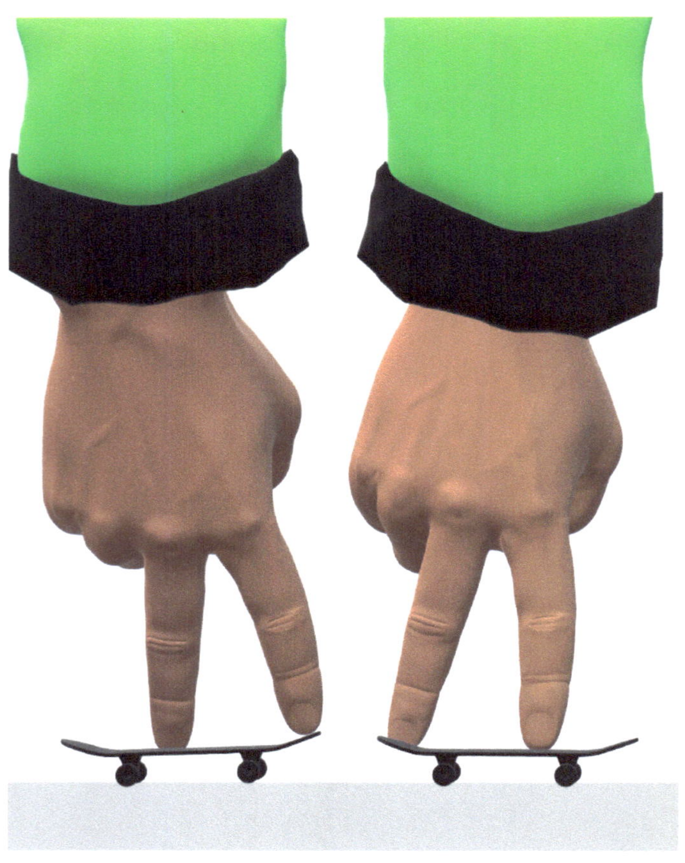

Pop Shuvs are another fun and fairly simple trick. The main difference between the Pop Shuv and a Shuv is the fact that Pop Shuvs get air.

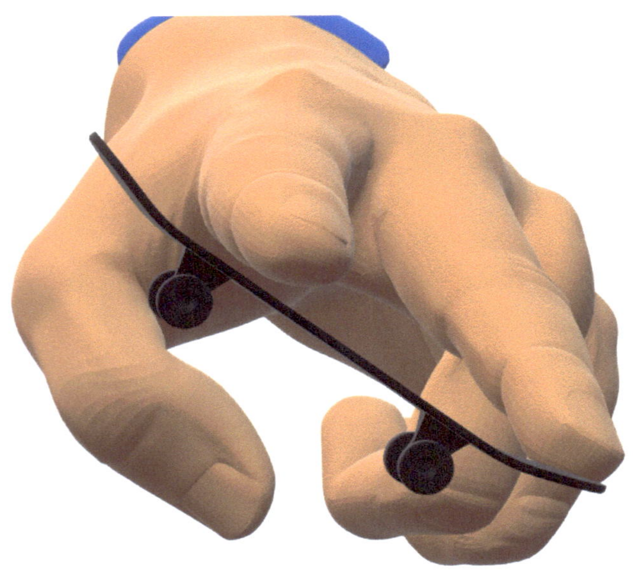

Pop Shuvs plus Kickflips/Heelflips create Varial Flips. Typically, Varial Flips are easier to do than Kickflips or Heelflips. Many people do them accidentally while trying to learn other tricks.

In time, tricks like Tre Flips, Hardflips, Dolphin Flips, and more will become doable. For some people, the transition from trick to trick is very easy, but other times, it is a process. Regardless of which one you are, learning the tricks is a fulfilling experience.

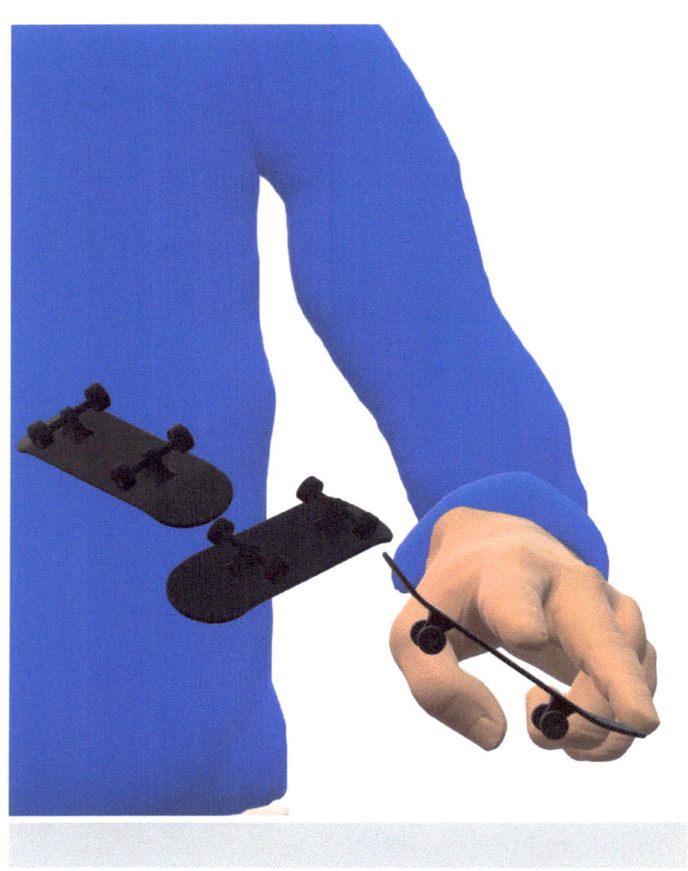

Impossibles are fun tricks to do, but they require commitment and practice. When you Ollie, the board wraps around your front and/or back finger. Initially, the board might make the motion of an Impossible without actually wrapping around your finger. Sometimes, the board will wrap around only your fingertip which might result in a strange-looking Impossible but an Impossible nonetheless. These tricks are not only fun; they also look pretty cool.

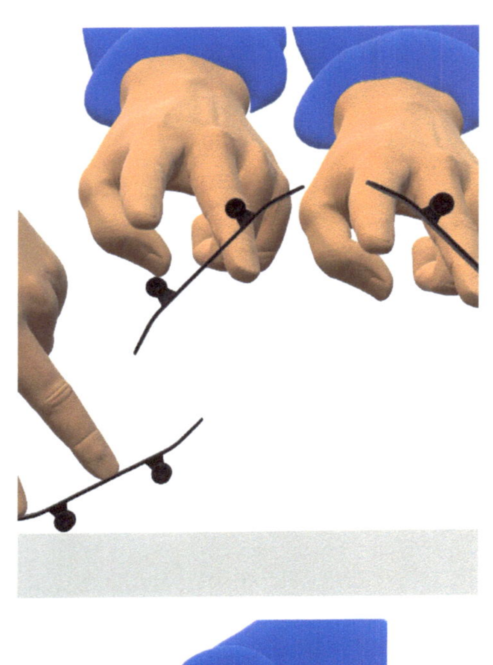

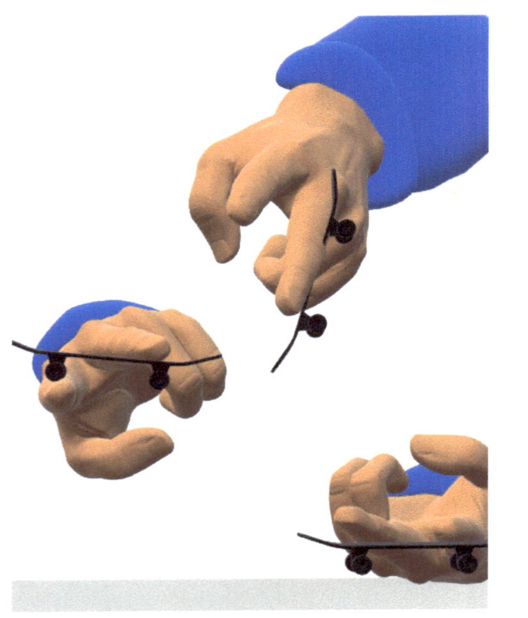

Doing an Ollie off of something is usually easier than doing an Ollie on to something, but learning how to Ollie on to objects is a great way to learn different grinds and slides.

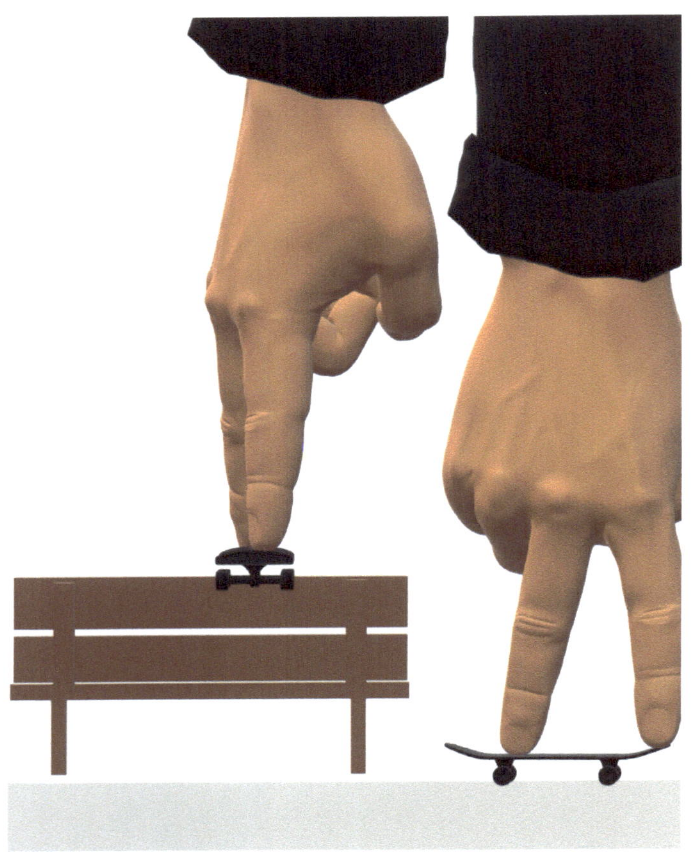

Fingerboarding accessories are very popular and can aid in the development of tricks and riding comfortably. For some people, fingerboarding with fingershoes is easier than fingerboarding without them. It does take some adjustment because the pressure that you have to put on the board is different. Also, catching the board with the shoes on is not always as easy as using your fingertips. Still, learning different ways to fingerboard is not a bad thing to do.

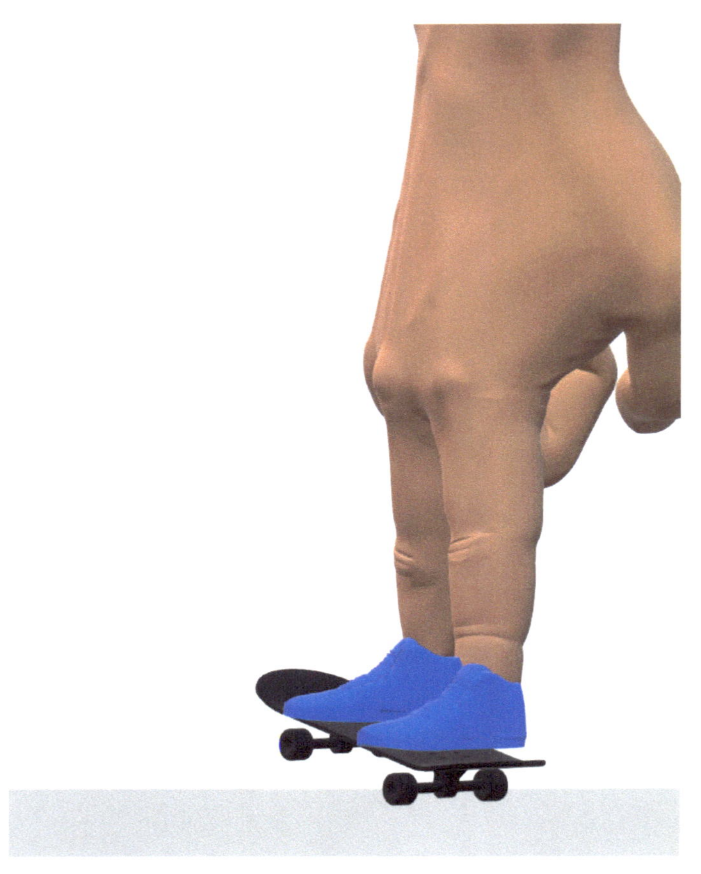

Although not everyone understands or supports fingerboarding, it is a lot of fun to do, and it can be a very inexpensive hobby depending on how you do it.

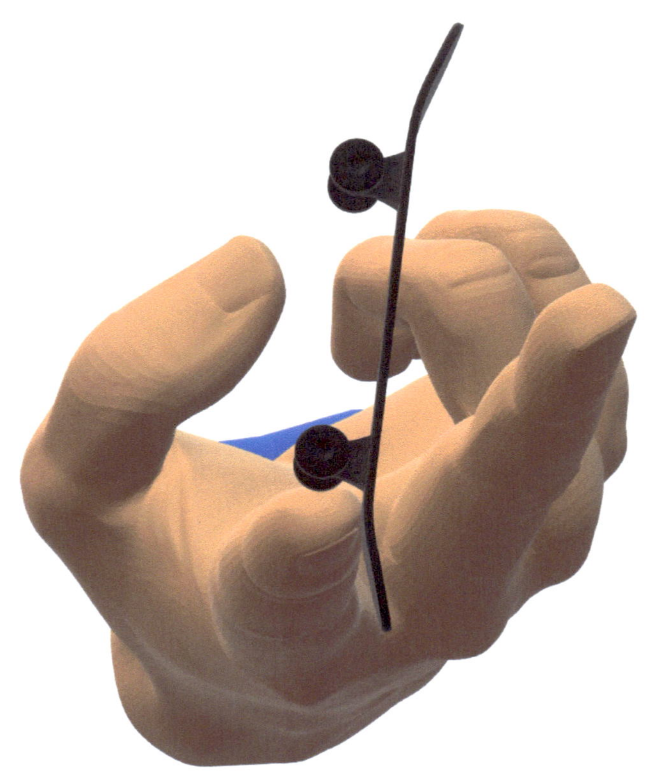

www.ingramcontent.com/pod-product-compliance
Lightning Source LLC
LaVergne TN
LVHW021309160826
845679LV00001B/278

* 9 7 9 8 3 6 8 0 7 1 5 1 0 *